WORDSWORTH'S
LAKE DISTRICT
THE LANDSCAPE AND ITS WRITERS

Rainbow over Coniston Water

My heart leaps up when I behold a rainbow in the sky:
So was it when my life began;
So is it now I am a man;
So be it when I shall grow old, or let me die!
The child is father of the man,
And I could wish my days to be
Bound each to each by natural piety.

The Rainbow   William Wordsworth

SALMON
An Ambassador Book

THE PICTURESQUE WRITERS

Derwentwater from Crow Park

Today the Lake District is famous across the world for its natural beauty, but until the late 18th Century this was a rarely visited, little known corner of England. From 1750 onwards a succession of writers published the first descriptions of the Lakeland scenery; these were the Picturesque Writers. The first to really capture the public's imagination was Dr. John Brown. In 1752 he proudly proclaimed,

"The full perfection of Keswick consists of three circumstances, Beauty, Horror and Immensity united". To give his readers an idea of this place which few had seen, he described Derwentwater in terms of the well-known Italian landscape painters. This was the essence of the Picturesque, not simply to turn *landscape* into *pictures*, but to compare *nature* to *art*.

Brown's letter was the best possible advert, establishing the Lake District, and Keswick in particular, as a tourist destination. Keswick at this time was already a busy little town, being the centre for the wool trade in the north Lakes, but over the next 30 years a visit to the Lakes became increasingly popular, attracting people like William Wilberforce and Thomas Gray.

The first true guidebook for the Lake District appeared in 1780, written by Thomas West of Ulverston. In his book, West directs visitors to all the best view points for each lake, which he calls "Stations". It was the fashion for the Picturesque Tourist to keep a diary of their visit and sketch the views, and West's Stations were recognised as the best places for artists to work. To reflect its supreme status, Derwentwater had eight Stations, many of which are still famous, including Crow Park, Castle Crag and Latrigg.

The most important Picturesque Writer was William Gilpin – writer, artist and art theorist. In 1786 he published his *Tour of the Lakes* in which he sets out his rules of picturesque beauty. Travelling on horseback along the east side of Derwentwater, Gilpin notes that the best picturesque views of the lake are to be found from the water's edge, in the many little bays. Continuing south, Gilpin arrived at the Jaws of Borrowdale, a spectacular gorge through which flow the crystalline waters of the River Derwent.

Borrowdale from Castle Crag

Beyond the Jaws, Borrowdale opens out to a wide fertile valley, overlooked by the mountains Glaramara and Great Gable. At the head of the valley is the tiny hamlet of Seathwaite which has the dubious honour of being the rainiest inhabited place in England. From Rosthwaite, Gilpin crossed the hills to the charming hamlet of Watendlath, which lies in a hidden valley above Derwentwater, then returned to Keswick past the now famous viewpoint at Ashness Bridge.

The early tourists were primarily interested in the lakes, but there was another good reason to visit Keswick. Rising dramatically above the town is Skiddaw, which was then believed to be England's highest mountain. The most adventurous of the early tourists could hire guides and ponies to take them to the summit. At a height of 3053ft, Skiddaw is now known to be England's fourth highest mountain, and the slate from which it is made is the oldest rock in Lakeland. With Keswick being so highly praised by the first Lakeland writers, it was perhaps only natural for the next generation, the Lake Poets, to come and settle here.

Ashness Bridge

THE LAKE POETS

Buttermere

The Lake Poets are now firmly connected with the Lake District, but their arrival in Keswick was almost accidental. Coleridge and Southey were both born in the West Country; they first met at Oxford, then became related by marrying sisters. When Wordsworth moved to Grasmere in 1799, Coleridge followed his new friend north to live at Greta Hall in Keswick. Greta Hall was large enough to accommodate two families and in 1803 the Southeys were also lured north to occupy the other half. By 1808 Coleridge's marriage had failed and he left Keswick, eventually to live in London, while Southey remained at Greta Hall, caring for both families.

Although he is little read today, Southey was, in his time, an important writer. He wrote on a wide range of subjects, including a biography of Nelson, a history of Brazil, and various translations (he translated the story of The Three Bears into English); and he was Poet Laureate from 1813 until his death in 1843. His best remembered poem was written for his children about Lodore Falls, the famous cascade on the east side of Derwentwater:

"... Around and around
With endless rebound!
Smiting and fighting,
A sight to delight in;
Confounding, astounding,
Dizzying and deafening the ear with its sound."

South-west of Keswick, the lake of Buttermere lies in deep seclusion between towering mountains; this is the setting for one of Lakeland's most famous tales. In 1802 Coleridge wrote a newspaper article reporting the marriage of a visiting MP, the Hon. Augustus Hope, to Mary Robinson, the famous Beauty of Buttermere. When the news reached Hope's family it was revealed that the real Hope was in India and the man in the Lakes must therefore be an impostor. He was arrested and his name discovered to be James Hatfield. Hatfield was later found to be a bigamist, but it was on charges of forgery that he was convicted and hanged in Carlisle.

Lodore Falls

Derwentwater and Keswick from Skiddaw

Wastwater and Great Gable

Coleridge's time in Lakeland was brief but spectacular. Although his best poetry had already been written, here he pioneered hill-walking, vividly recording his experiences in his notebooks. His favourite hill was almost certainly Blencathra which towers impressively above the village of Threlkeld, east of Keswick.

"On stern Blencathra's perilous height
The winds are tyrannous and strong;
And flashing forth unsteady light
From stern Blencathra's skiey height
As loud the torrents throng ..."

In the summer of 1802 Coleridge set out on a ten-day walking tour of western Lakeland, visiting Buttermere, Ennerdale and the Cumbrian coast. After four days he arrived at the remote lake of Wastwater. In his notebooks Coleridge struggled to find words to capture the scenery. Wastwater is the most dramatic of the lakes: on the eastern shore screes of huge boulders plunge more than 2000ft to the bottom of the lake, and at the head of the

View north from Scafell

valley stands the pyramid-shaped Great Gable. Coleridge spent the night at Wasdale Head, then in the morning he started off into the hills for the long climb up Scafell (3162ft), England's second highest mountain. At the top he wrote:

"Oh my God! What enormous mountains these are, close by me and yet below the hill I stand on... But Oh! What a look down just under my feet! The frightfullest cove that might ever be seen: huge perpendicular precipices and one sheep upon its only ledge... Just by it and joining together, rise two huge pillars of bare, lead-coloured stone; I am no measurer but their height and depth is terrible."

Coleridge then made a death-defying descent by a route known as Broad Stand which involved slithering down sheer rock-faces.

Blencathra from St. John's Vale

WILLIAM WORDSWORTH

Wordsworth House, Cockermouth

Unlike many other Lakeland writers, William Wordsworth was born and raised in the area which was to be his inspiration and home for much of his 80-year life. He was born in Cockermouth on 7ᵗʰ April 1770, the second of four brothers with the only sister, Dorothy, born on Christmas Day the following year. His birthplace stands at the west end of Main Street, a suitably grand residence for Wordsworth's father, who held a good position from Sir James Lowther, then the richest man in northern England.

William had fond memories of the River Derwent; it gave him his first experiences of nature, and it became a childhood playground. Today there are delightful walks by the river with views of the castle, where William also played as a child.

The Wordsworth children spent much of their early life at Penrith in the care of relatives; it was here that William first met his future wife, Mary Hutchinson. The town is dominated by its ruined castle, which dates back to the 14th century and, like many of Penrith's older buildings, is built from a distinctive red sandstone. Stretching to the south-east of Penrith is the beautiful Eden Valley, which forms Lakeland's eastern boundary with the Pennines.

Cockermouth is a busy market town on the north-west edge of the Lake District. The name is derived from the River Cocker, which meets the Derwent just outside the town and flows behind Wordsworth House.

Penrith Castle

River Derwent, Cockermouth

"... When, having left his mountains, to the Towers
Of Cockermouth that beauteous river came,
Behind my father's house he passed, close by ...

... the fairest of all rivers, loved
To blend his murmurs with my nurse's song,
And from his alder shades and rocky falls,
And from his fords and shallows, sent a voice
That flowed along my dreams ..."

Standing five miles south of Ambleside is Hawkshead. This is a favourite place for today's visitors, famous for its whitewashed houses and teashops. Before the reorganisation of the counties in 1974, the whole area west of Windermere as far as the Duddon Valley, including Hawkshead and Coniston, was part of Lancashire. In Wordsworth's time Hawkshead was a busy village, well placed near the junction of roads to Ambleside, Coniston and the Windermere Ferry.

In 1779 William and his brothers were sent here to attend the Grammar School; the building is open to the public and can be found at the south end of the village, below the church. The house where William and his brothers lodged can also be found on what is now called Wordsworth Street – perhaps less quaint than its former name of Leather, Rag and Putty Street – at the north end of the village. William's headmaster encouraged him to read and write poetry; this kindled his interest at an early age.

The school's timetable was demanding. In summer, school began at 6:30am, but there was still time for "boyish pursuits" – fishing, horse riding, boating, ice-skating and exploring, especially around Hawkshead's own little lake, Esthwaite Water, which lies half a mile to the south.

Hawkshead Church

Hawkshead Grammar School

"Beloved Hawkshead . . . thy paths, thy shores
And brooks, were like a dream of novelty
To my half-infant mind . . .
. . . My morning walks
Were early: oft before the hours of school
I travelled round our little lake, five miles
Of pleasant wandering – happy time . . ."

Esthwaite Water

One of William's walks from Hawkshead brought him within sight of Grasmere and left him with a memorable impression of the lake and vale which he recalls in *Home at Grasmere:*

"... *thy crags, and woody steeps, thy Lake,*
Its one green Island and its winding shores,
The multitude of little rocky hills,
Thy Church and Cottages of mountain stone –
Clustered like stars ..."

In 1787 William finished school and left the Lake District for the first time to attend Cambridge University. For the next 10 years he lived mainly in the south of England, but in 1799 he decided he needed to be amongst his native mountains and he chose to live in Grasmere Vale.

Grasmere from Loughrigg

Dove Cottage

Dove Cottage stands in the hamlet of Town End, half a mile south of Grasmere village. The building had previously been an inn, on what was then the main road through the Lakes. William Wordsworth and his sister Dorothy moved in on 20th December 1799. Now with the stability of a private income, William was able to concentrate on poetry, and many of his most famous poems were written here.

Dorothy also wrote; she kept a diary, *The Grasmere Journals,* in which she recorded their daily lives and her observations of nature. The 8½ years at Dove Cottage were happy times for the Wordsworths; in 1802 William married Mary Hutchinson and they began their family life here.

The area around Dove Cottage was dearly loved by the Wordsworths, and gave them great pleasure on their daily walks. According to Dorothy, "our favourite path" led onto White Moss Common, a low ridge of open hillside between the lakes of Grasmere and Rydal, with good views of both. Dorothy describes White Moss Common in her *Journals:*

Rydal Water from White Moss Common

"...a place made for all kinds of beautiful works of art, and nature, woods and valleys,
fairy valleys and fairy tarns, miniature mountains, alps above alps..."

Daffodils at Gowbarrow, Ullswater

I wandered lonely as a cloud
That floats on high o'er vales and hills,
When all at once I saw a crowd,
A host of golden daffodils;
Beside the lake, beneath the trees,
Fluttering and dancing in the breeze.

Continuous as the stars that shine
And twinkle on the milky way,
They stretched in never-ending line
Along the margin of the bay:
Ten thousand saw I at a glance
Tossing their heads in sprightly dance.

The waves beside them danced; but they
Out-did the sparkling waves in glee:
A poet could not but be gay,
In such a jocund company;
I gazed - and gazed — but little thought
What wealth the show to me had brought:

For oft, when on my couch I lie
In vacant or in pensive mood,
They flash upon that inward eye
Which is the bliss of solitude;
And then my heart with pleasure fills,
And dances with the daffodils.

Ullswater is the second - largest lake in the Lake District, stretching north-east from Patterdale out towards Penrith. On 15th April 1802, William and Dorothy were walking along the north shore towards Glenridding, and Dorothy recorded the things they saw in her *Journals*:

"When we were in the woods beyond Gowbarrow Park we saw a few daffodils close to the water-side. We fancied that the lake had floated the seeds ashore, and that the little colony had so sprung up. But as we went along there were more and yet more; and at last, under the boughs of the trees, we saw that there was a long belt of them along the shore, about the breadth of a country turnpike road. I never saw daffodils so beautiful. They grew among the mossy stones about and about them; some rested their heads upon these stones as on a pillow for weariness; and the rest tossed and reeled and danced, and seemed as if they verily laughed with the wind, that blew upon them over the lake; they looked so gay, ever glancing, ever changing. There was here and there a little knot, and a few stragglers a few yards higher up; but they were so few as not to disturb the simplicity, unity, and life of that one busy highway."

Aira Force

Ullswater from Gowbarrow Fell

Although the details are not recorded, this almost certainly gave William the central image of his most famous poem. Today, the north shore of Ullswater near Gowbarrow Park is still one of the best places to see wild daffodils.

Gowbarrow Park is also home to the mountain stream of Aira Beck, as it tumbles down to Ullswater. This is the setting for Wordsworth's poems *The Somnambulist* and *Airey-Force Valley*. The falls and the surrounding area are owned by the National Trust. The paths and bridges around the falls were constructed during Victorian times.

Wordsworth had an intimate knowledge of the Lake District and felt that the best way to explore was on foot. One excursion he specifically recommends in his *Guide to the Lakes* is a circuit of the Langdale valleys (Little and Great Langdale), west of Ambleside. In his time this would have to be walked, but can now be done by car. Dominating the landscape here and for many miles around are the famous Langdale Pikes, one of Lakeland's most distinctive mountain skylines.

Beyond the head of Langdale, between the valleys of Borrowdale and Wasdale, rises a massive ridge of volcanic rock. These are the Scafells; the highest point, Scafell Pike (3210ft), is England's highest mountain. In his *Guide to the Lakes,* Wordsworth records a visit to the summit:

"We now beheld the whole mass of Great Gable from its base, – the Den of Wasdale at our feet – a gulf immeasurable… Around the top of Scafell Pike not a blade of grass is to be seen. Cushions or tufts of moss, parched and brown, appear between the huge blocks and stones that lie in heaps on all sides to a great distance, like skeletons or bones of the earth not needed at the creation".

Langdale and the Langdale Pikes

Great Gable from Scafell Pike

Wordsworth's favourite mountain was almost certainly Helvellyn, which towers above the east side of Thirlmere. At a height of 3118ft, this is England's third-highest mountain, and a favourite amongst walkers with its knife-like ridges of Striding Edge and Swirral Edge. In *Fidelity,* Wordsworth captures the changing moods of this mighty mountain and of Red Tarn which lies below the summit.

"Thither the rainbow comes — the cloud —
And mists that spread the flying shroud;
And sunbeams; and the sounding blast,
That, if it could, would hurry past;
But that enormous barrier holds it fast."

Helvellyn from Thirlmere

In 1813 the Wordsworth family moved to Rydal Mount in the small village of Rydal, between Ambleside and Grasmere; this was to be their home for the rest of their lives. The extensive gardens enjoy fine views across the surrounding landscape, and here Wordsworth constructed terrace walks where he could compose poetry. At Rydal Mount, Wordsworth finally received public acclaim for his poetry with the *Duddon Sonnets* (published 1820), and for his *Guide to the Lakes*. He also campaigned on many issues, most famously working against the Windermere Railway, which was planned to run through Rydal and Grasmere to Keswick.

In his *Guide to the Lakes,* Wordsworth defended Lakeland against aggressive change and called it "a sort of national property", which foresaw the establishment of the National Park by more than 100 years. In 1843 he became Poet Laureate to Queen Victoria.

In 1825 Wordsworth bought a plot of land beside Rydal Church which he later gave to his daughter, Dora; it has ever since been known as Dora's Field. One of Wordsworth's poems is carved into a rock here and, in the spring, Dora's Field is famous for its display of bluebells and daffodils.

Rydal Mount

Dora's Field

"...yon gracious church,
That has a look so full of peace and hope
And love — benignant Mother of the Vale,
How fair amid her brood of cottages!..."

Wordsworth died at Rydal on 23rd April 1850, and he was buried in a corner of Grasmere churchyard, overlooking the River Rothay. The church itself dates from the 13th century and is dedicated to St. Oswald. Inside there is a memorial plaque to Wordsworth. Every summer Grasmere holds its Rushbearing Ceremony, a tradition stemming from the time before the church's stone floor, when the original beaten earth floor would be covered with a layer of rushes. Every year fresh rushes were cut at the lake-shore and brought to the church in a procession through the village. Although the church has been paved since Victorian times, the ceremony has continued, as it does in Ambleside and other places in northern England.

Grasmere Church

JOHN RUSKIN

Friar's Crag, Derwentwater

John Ruskin professed his earliest memory to be of the Lake District. At the age of five, his nurse had taken him to the tip of Friar's Crag, a rocky outcrop protruding from the shore of Derwentwater; an experience which left with him a lasting impression of "intense joy mingled with awe". Born in London in 1819, Ruskin studied at Oxford University, and shortly after graduating published the first volume of *Modern Painters*, his first great work of criticism which would span several volumes. This was begun largely in defence of the artist JMW Turner – who had been fiercely attacked by the art establishment for his later style of painting – and of the landscape painters in general. In his second volume, Ruskin proceeded to write another controversial defence, this time of the pre-Raphaelite painters.

The first appearance of *Modern Painters* established Ruskin's reputation, and he went on to write several major works of criticism, most notably *The Seven Lamps of Architecture* (1849) and *The Stones of Venice* (1853). He also became an inspiration for the emerging Arts and Crafts movement, who shared his repugnance for mass-production with its degradation of the craftsman. But Ruskin was much more than an art critic. Himself one of the greatest Victorian watercolourists, he was appointed Slade Professor of Art at Oxford University; he was a political economist and advocate of social reform; and he was an avid student of geology and natural history.

As a boy, Ruskin had been profoundly affected by his first visit to the Alps, and frequently returned to them throughout his life. He later compared their beauty to the "walls of lost Eden"; and here in the Lake District he found a similar landscape to inspire him. Ruskin came to Brantwood on the eastern shore of Coniston Water in 1872. It was then a modest house, on which he would imprint his own ideas of design and architecture. His first addition to the building was the tiny turret room that looks out over the lake to the Coniston Fells, from where he could enjoy what he had described as "the finest view I know in Cumberland or Lancashire". Today, visitors can enjoy the very same spectacular views, as the house is now a museum dedicated to Ruskin's life and work.

Ruskin is buried in Coniston churchyard, his grave marked by a fine Celtic-style cross; whilst on Friar's Crag stands a memorial – designed by WG Collingwood, Ruskin's long-time secretary and disciple – to perhaps the most eminent of Victorian writers.

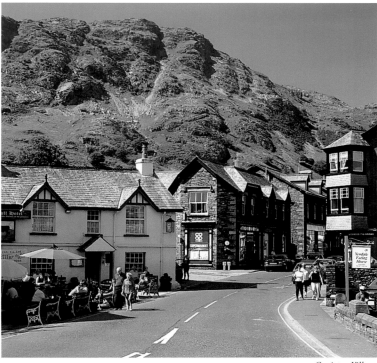

Coniston Village

Brantwood, Coniston Water

BEATRIX POTTER

Wray Castle, Windermere

Beatrix Potter was approaching her sixteenth birthday when she first visited the Lake District. Her father, a wealthy London barrister, was in the habit of renting large country houses for the family's long summer holidays. Earlier summers had been spent in Scotland, but in 1882 the Potters took the mock-gothic mansion Wray Castle, on Lake Windermere, as their temporary residence. This was Beatrix's first introduction to the area which was to become her literary and artistic inspiration, and her adopted home.

In the following years, the Lake District became a regular holiday destination for the Potter family. Wray Castle was succeeded by Lingholm and Fawe Park, both large houses on the western shores of Derwentwater; Holehird near Windermere; and later Lakefield (renamed Eeswyke) in the village of Sawrey. Beatrix and her brother would take their menagerie of pet animals on holiday with them, and would spend their time exploring and collecting and drawing the local wildlife. And throughout these long summer holidays and shorter trips to the south coast and West Country, Beatrix recorded scenes and impressions - in her sketchbooks and journal as well as in the illustrated letters that she wrote to children – which would later provide source material for her books.

Newlands Valley

St. Herbert's Island, Derwentwater

Derwentwater became the setting for her first Lakeland book, *The Tale of Squirrel Nutkin,* in which the woods along the lakeshore are the haunt of Squirrel Nutkin and his friends. St Herbert's Island, named after the seventh-century hermit-saint who once lived within its confines, for Beatrix becomes Owl Island, home to a rather different reclusive character, Old Brown.

Lying just a few miles to the west of Derwentwater is the beautiful Newlands Valley, home to Mrs Tiggy-Winkle. It was while staying at Lingholm that the Potters became acquainted with the Vicar of Newlands, and it was for his daughter, Lucie, that *The Tale of Mrs Tiggy-Winkle* was written. Little-town, Lucie's home, still shelters under the side of the humpbacked hill Cat Bells; and the paths that wind along the valley above the cottages are still to be found – just as they appear in Beatrix's drawings.

As the years passed, Beatrix grew evermore attached to the Lakeland landscape and way of life, and in 1905 she purchased her first Lake District property, Hill Top Farm in the village of Near Sawrey, two miles south of Hawkshead. The sales of her first five books had been phenomenal – *The Tale of Peter Rabbit* had sold fifty thousand copies in the first two years – and the farm was paid for by the royalties from the books together with a modest legacy.

Hill Top remained a working farm, and Beatrix took an active role in its management. Although she continued to live with her parents, who were often reluctant to spare her from the London home, she found the time to visit her beloved Hill Top whenever she could. She had a new wing added to the farmhouse to accommodate John Cannon, the sitting tenant who was kept on to run the farm and care for her animals in her absence; and the old house she filled with her many treasured possessions.

Beatrix made use of the traditional farmhouse interior and cottage garden, as well as the countryside round about, in her illustrations. Hill Top is home to Tom Kitten and his family, to Samuel Whiskers and to Jemima Puddleduck, while the village of Near Sawrey is populated by a host of other familiar characters. At least nine of the stories are set in and around the quaint villages of Sawrey and Hawkshead or in the surrounding countryside, and they are illustrated with scenes that can still be recognised today.

Hill Top, Sawrey

Buckle Yeat, Sawrey

View over Sawrey

Esthwaite Water

Lying between the villages of Near Sawrey and Hawkshead is Esthwaite Water, often sketched by Beatrix. With its reedy shallows and green flotillas of lily pads, Esthwaite provided a backdrop for some of her illustrations for *The Tale of Mr. Jeremy Fisher,* which was published within a year of her purchase of Hill Top. Another possible source of backgrounds for this book is Moss Eccles Tarn, perhaps the most beautiful of a number of small tarns which sit above Sawrey on the high ground between Esthwaite Water and Windermere. Moss Eccles Tarn became a favourite place, where Beatrix kept a rowing boat (now in the collection of the Windermere Steamboat Museum).

It was in 1913, on her marriage to the Hawkshead solicitor William Heelis, that Beatrix finally and permanently settled in her beloved Lake District. In 1909 she had bought her second farm in Near Sawrey, Castle Farm, and it was here that she lived until her death in 1943, while Hill Top she kept as her private retreat and workplace. Following her marriage, Beatrix immersed herself in country life, devoting more and more of her time to farming and gradually acquiring more and more land. She used her husband's law firm in her property dealings, and was a frequent visitor to his office in Hawkshead – which is now a National Trust museum housing a display of her original paintings.

Castle Farm, near Sawrey

Beatrix Potter Gallery, Hawkshead

Troutbeck Park Farm

Beatrix's increasing dedication to farming arose out of the conviction that the Lakeland landscape and way of life that she loved so dearly was under threat from encroaching development, and that the only way to protect it was by owning and responsibly farming the land. When she purchased Troutbeck Park Farm in 1924, she acquired along with its 2000 acres a flock of hundreds of Herdwick sheep; this was the start of her association with the Lake District's hardy native sheep breed.

Legend says that the Herdwick arrived in Cumbria in the 10th century when a flock of 40 sheep survived a shipwreck. This may be possible, as the name is of Norse origin; but however they arrived, they are certainly well suited to the harsh conditions and poor grazing on the Lakeland fells. Beatrix became a highly successful sheep breeder, winning prizes for her Herdwicks at the local agricultural shows and ultimately being elected President of the Herdwick Sheepbreeders' Association – a great honour in Cumbrian farming circles.

Yew Tree Farm

Herdwick sheep in Langdale

Beatrix's determination to protect the Lake District lead her to work ever more closely with The National Trust. When the huge Monk Coniston estate came up for sale in 1929, Beatrix bought the whole property – consisting of some 4000 acres between Little Langdale and Coniston and including the popular beauty spot of Tarn Hows along with several farms – immediately selling on half to The National Trust at cost whilst keeping the remainder for her lifetime.

When she died at Castle Farm in 1943, Beatrix left a total of 15 farms and 4000 acres of land to the care of The National Trust; so ensuring the survival of the landscape that she loved and that had inspired so much of her work.

ARTHUR RANSOME

Coniston Water from near Nibthwaite

Arthur Ransome was born in 1884 in Leeds where his father worked as a college lecturer; but the Ransomes had Cumbrian connections. Arthur's father had been born in Cumbria, and every year the family returned to the Lakes for their holidays. They usually stayed at High Nibthwaite at the southern end of Coniston Water, and it was here that the young Arthur Ransome learned about fishing, camping and sailing – activities which would later become the basic ingredients for his *Swallows and Amazons* books.

The lake of *The Swallows and Amazons* cannot be found on maps, but was instead carefully constructed by Ransome from favourite parts of both Coniston and Windermere, which he rearranged and renamed. Soon after their publication, Ransome's books proved immensely popular and many of his readers wanted to find the original settings; but Ransome always kept these secret. Over many years though, researchers have been able to identify most of the locations, both actual and composite. Perhaps the most important of these is Peel Island on Coniston Water, just a mile up the lake from Nibthwaite. Rechristened Wild Cat Island, this becomes the hub of the action of *The Swallows and Amazons,* claimed and contested by both sets of children as their camp. To the west of the lake the Old Man of Coniston dominates the skyline; this is the peak Kanchenjunga which is climbed by the Swallows in the second book, *Swallowdale.*

Perhaps the best way to see Coniston Water is from the decks of the steam yacht *Gondola,* which carries passengers up and down the lake in perfect Victorian elegance. The *Gondola* has often been mistaken for Captain Flint's Houseboat, being very similar to Ransome's illustrations. However, a stronger contender for this honour is the steam yacht *Esperance,* which can now be found – along with the original *Amazon* – beautifully preserved at the Windermere Steamboat Museum near Bowness.

Bank Ground Farm and Coniston Water

The Gondola, Coniston Water

Windermere and Bowness from Claife Heights

At more than 10 miles in length, Windermere is the largest natural lake in England. Stretching from the mountainous landscape around Ambleside to the gentler countryside to the south towards Newby Bridge, its array of islands and secluded bays make it ideal for boating. Situated midway along its eastern shore is the busy town of Bowness. Little more than a village until the 1840s, Bowness owes its establishment as a major tourist destination to the arrival of the railway at nearby Windermere town, and to this day it retains much of its character as a Victorian resort. Bowness features in *Swallows and Amazons* as Rio, a haven for sailing boats and pleasure craft of all descriptions.

Bowness-on-Windermere

Waterhead, Ambleside

Ransome's connection with this part of the Lake District stems from his early schooldays, when he attended a boarding school in Windermere. His fondest schoolday memories were of the Great Frost of 1895 when the lake froze for a whole month and the boys were allowed to spend day after day playing on the ice. In 1925, after an already eventful career as a foreign correspondent and writer, Ransome came to live in the Winster Valley, a few miles to the east of Windermere. This heralded the most productive period for his writing, and it was here in 1929 that he began to write the *Swallows and Amazons* books. The fourth of the series, *Winter Holiday*, is the book most firmly set in the Windermere landscape. Recalling Ransome's own memories of both the Great Frost of 1895 and the winter of 1929 when again the lake froze, in *Winter Holiday* the children plan an expedition across the frozen lake, skating north to Waterhead which they imagine to be an Eskimo settlement at the North Pole.

One of the most enduring puzzles of Ransome's Lakeland must be the true location of Swallowdale, the Swallows' mountain camp of the second *Swallows and Amazons* book. The most likely location is on Blawith Common at the southern end of Coniston Water, where the real Swallowdale can be found in exactly the same way as it was discovered by the Swallows – by following a stream from the lakeshore up into the hills.

The River Crake, which flows southwards out of Coniston Water and through Allan Tarn (known to the Swallows as Octopus Lagoon) before passing by the village of Nibthwaite, was well-loved by Ransome as a boy. It becomes the model for his River Amazon which, in the altered geography of the stories, flows *into* the lake near the Amazons' home at Beckfoot, rather than out of the lake's southernmost end as it does in real life.

Further upstream, the fictional River Amazon is a rocky mountain beck, which Ransome modelled on Tilberthwaite Gill, north of Coniston. This stretch of the river becomes the central location of the book *Pigeon Post*, where the children again set up camp in the hills, this time in order to go prospecting for gold. Again, Ransome has carefully created an altered version of the real landscape. The hills above Tilberthwaite were once an important site for copper mining and slate quarrying, and the surface remains of many

Coniston Water from Blawith Common

of these mines and quarries still litter the hillside. The quest for gold takes the incautious children underground into the abandoned mines: this is an extremely dangerous activity which cannot be recommended – as the children discover when they narrowly escape being entombed by a cave-in.

Arthur Ransome died in 1967 and is buried in Rusland churchyard, close to his final home. Although he had spent a number of years living in Suffolk – with a further five of his twelve children's adventures set on the Norfolk Broads – it was to the Lake District that he returned. Like the Lakeland writers who went before him, Ransome's books show the profound influence of a landscape that not only inspired but became a part of his fictional world; and like them, he will forever be associated with some of the most beautiful and dramatic scenery to be found in Britain.

Tilberthwaite Gill

Cathedral Cave, Little Langdale

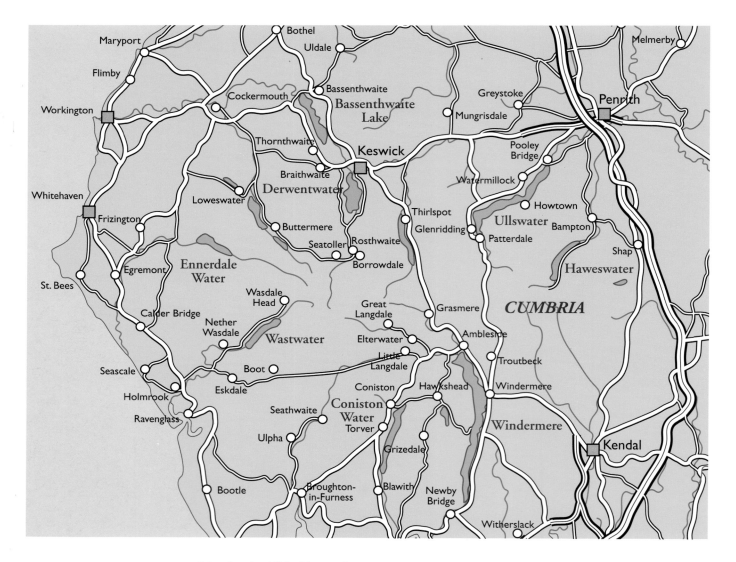

Printed and published by J. Salmon Ltd., Sevenoaks, Kent TN13 1BB

Designed by the Salmon Studio. Copyright © 2001 J. Salmon Ltd.

Photographs copyright © Alex Black Text copyright © Hazel Gatford

ISBN 1 902842 24 3

Cover picture: Grasmere from Loughrigg   *Back cover:* Daffodils at Gowbarrow, Ullswater